The Perks of Being a Wallflower

Classroom Questions & Comparative Study Questions

A SCENE BY SCENE TEACHING GUIDE

Amy Farrell

SCENE BY SCENE
ENNISKERRY, IRELAND

Copyright © 2017 by Scene by Scene.

Without limiting the rights under copyright, this book is sold subject to the condition that it shall not, by way of trade or otherwise be lent, resold, hired out, reproduced, stored on or introduced into a retrieval system, or transmitted, in any form or by any means (electronic, mechanical, photocopying, recording or otherwise), or otherwise circulated, without the publisher's prior consent, in any form other than that in which it is published and without a similar condition, including this condition, being imposed on the subsequent publisher.

All rights reserved. No part of this publication may be recorded or transmitted in any form or by any means electronic, mechanical, photocopying, recording or otherwise without the proper consent of the publisher.

The publisher reserves the right to change, without notice, at any time, the specification of this product, whether by change of materials, colours, format, text revision or any other characteristic.

Scene by Scene
Enniskerry
Wicklow, Ireland.
www.scenebysceneguides.com

The Perks of Being a Wallflower Classroom Questions by Amy Farrell.
ISBN 978-1-910949-61-0

Contents

Letter One (August 25, 1991)   1

Letter Two (September 7, 1991)   5

Letter Three (September 11, 1991)   7

Letter Four (September 16, 1991)   9

Letter Five (September 18, 1991)   11

Letter Six (September 29, 1991)   13

Letter Seven (October 6, 1991)   15

Letter Eight (October 14, 1991)   17

Letter Nine (October 15, 1991)   21

Letter Ten (October 28, 1991)   23

Letter Eleven (November 7, 1991)   27

Letter Twelve (November 8, 1991)   29

Letter Thirteen (November 12, 1991)   31

Letter Fourteen (November 15, 1991)   33

Letter Fifteen (November 18, 1991)   35

Letter Sixteen (November 23, 1991)   37

Letter Seventeen (December 7, 1991)   41

Letter Eighteen (December 11, 1991)   43

Letter Nineteen (December 19, 1991)   45

Letter Twenty (December 21, 1991)   47

Letter Twenty-One (December 23, 1991)   51

Letter Twenty-Two (December 25, 1991)   53

Letter Twenty-Three (December 26, 1991)	58
Letter Twenty-Four (December 30, 1991)	62
Letter Twenty-Five (January 1, 1992)	64
Letter Twenty-Six (January 4, 1992)	66
Letter Twenty-Seven (January 14, 1992)	69
Letter Twenty-Eight (January 25, 1992)	71
Letter Twenty-Nine (February 2, 1992)	73
Letter Thirty (February 8, 1992)	75
Letter Thirty-One (February 9, 1992)	77
Letter Thirty-Two (February 15, 1992)	79
Letter Thirty-Three (February 23, 1992)	81
Letter Thirty-Four (March 7, 1992)	84
Letter Thirty-Five (March 28, 1992)	86
Letter Thirty-Six (April 18, 1992)	88
Letter Thirty-Seven (April 26, 1992)	92
Letter Thirty-Eight (April 29, 1992)	94
Letter Thirty-Nine (May 2, 1992)	96
Letter Forty (May 8, 1992)	98
Letter Forty-One (May 11, 1992)	102
Letter Forty-Two (May 17, 1992)	104
Letter Forty-Three (May 21, 1992)	106
Letter Forty-Four (May 27, 1992)	108
Letter Forty-Five (June 2, 1992)	110
Letter Forty-Six (June 5, 1992)	112
Letter Forty-Seven (June 9, 1992)	114
Letter Forty-Eight (June 10, 1992)	116

Letter Forty-Nine (June 13, 1992)	118
Letter Fifty (June 16, 1992)	121
Letter Fifty-One (June 22, 1992)	125
Epilogue: Letter Fifty-Two (August 23, 1992)	129
Further Questions	133
Theme/Issue (HL) ~ Relationships (OL)	135
Literary Genre (HL)	140
General Vision and Viewpoint (HL)	145
Cultural Context (HL)/Social Setting (OL)	151
Hero, Heroine, Villain (OL)	156
The Comparative Study: Comparing Texts	158

Letter One (August 25, 1991)

Summary

The speaker, Charlie, writes this letter hoping that the recipient will listen and understand.

Charlie's friend, Michael, killed himself. When it happened, Charlie's older brother came and got him from school.

In the counselor sessions, Charlie got very upset, crying and screaming at the counselor. After this the teachers treated Charlie differently, and gave him better grades than he deserved.

Charlie finds it strange that Michael's father did not cry at the funeral. He wonders about Michael's home and wishes he knew what went on, so that he can make some sense of it.

Charlie describes his family. He is the youngest of three children. His aunt Helen, his favourite person, lived her final years with his family because something very bad happened to her. She would not tell Charlie what this was.

He stopped asking her when he was seven. She got upset and Charlie's dad slapped him.

The reason why Charlie is writing this letter is because he is starting high school tomorrow and is afraid of going.

Questions

1. Why is the speaker writing this letter?
   What does this tell you about the speaker?

2. What happened to Michael, the speaker's friend?

3. How does the speaker's older brother treat him when he comes to Mr Vaughn's office?

4. What really bothered Charlie about Michael's death?

5. How does Charlie behave during the session with the counselors?
   What makes him act this way?

6. What did Charlie find strange about Michael's funeral?
   Do you agree with him here?

7. Describe Charlie's family.
   Is there anything in particular that strikes you about them?

8. Did Charlie have a good relationship with his aunt Helen?

9. Why did his aunt Helen live with Charlie's family?

10. What reason does Charlie give for writing this letter before he signs off?
    What is your response to this?
    Why doesn't he talk to someone?

11. What questions do you have after reading this first chapter?

12. What are your first impressions of Charlie, based on this chapter?

13. What is the tone of this opening chapter?

14. What do you expect this novel to be about?

Letter Two (September 7, 1991)

Summary

Charlie does not like high school.

Susan, a girl who went out with Michael, has changed over the summer. She acts a lot dumber now, especially around boys.

A boy called Sean says he will give Charlie a "swirlie" and Charlie fights with him, really hurting him.

Charlie is upset afterwards and his sister has to drive him home. He does not get in trouble because Sean started it.

Charlie is lonely as his older siblings are busy. He needs to work hard to get a college scholarship, so that is what he is doing until he makes a friend.

Questions

1. How has Susan changed over the summer?

2. Why does Charlie really hurt Sean?
   Do you feel sorry for Sean here?

3. How does Charlie react to the fight?
   Why is this the case, do you think?

4. Why has it been very lonely for Charlie?

5. Why must Charlie work hard at school?

6. Read the last paragraph of this letter again.
   How does it add to your impression of Charlie?

Letter Three (September 11, 1991)

Summary

Charlie does not have a lot of free time as he is reading *To Kill a Mockingbird* for class.

He saw his brother playing football on television. Charlie misses him terribly.

Questions

1. Charlie talks about his preferred reading methods in this letter.
   How do you like to read?
   Do you like being assigned a few chapters at a time?

2. Why is Charlie writing this letter?

3. What does Charlie think is strange?

4. Why doesn't Charlie mention the position his brother plays?
   Is this a good strategy, do you think?

Letter Four (September 16, 1991)

Summary

Charlie loves *To Kill a Mockingbird*. His advanced english teacher, Bill, is impressed with him.

His sister gives him a mix tape a boy made her. Charlie loves it. His sister is mean to this boy and makes him cry one night, saying he did not stand up to a bully.

The boy hits Charlie's sister. His sister does not do anything in return. Later on, she says that she is going out with this boy now.

At the weekend, Charlie accidentally walks in on his sister and this boy having sex.

The next day the boy comes over to watch Charlie's brother playing football on television. Charlie's parents like him.

Charlie feels bad for his sister and her boyfriend.

Questions

1. How is Charlie getting on in advanced english?

2. Charlie says his sister is really mean to the boys she meets. Do you agree with him here?

3. Why does the boy hit Charlie's sister?
   What is your response to this?
   What would you do, if you were Charlie?

4. How does Charlie's sister react to the boy hitting her?
   What makes her react this way, do you think?

5. What does Charlie walk in on in the basement?
   How would you feel if you were Charlie?

6. How do Charlie's parents feel about his sister's boyfriend?

7. At the end of this letter, Charlie says that he feels very bad for his sister and her boyfriend.
   Why is this, do you think?

8. What insight into the world of the story does this letter provide?

9. Do you think this is a realistic portrayal of teenagers' lives?
   Refer to the text to support your point of view.

Letter Five (September 18, 1991)

Summary

There is a hilarious guy in Charlie's shop class called Nothing (his real name is Patrick).

Charlie's sister asked for her mix tape back and listens to it all the time.

Questions

1. How did "Nothing" get his name?

2. What is Nothing like?

3. What is the significance of Charlie's sister wanting the mix tape back?

4. Is there a present day equivalent of a 'mix tape'?

5. Why do people make 'mix tapes'?

Letter Six (September 29, 1991)

Summary

Charlie is working for advanced english, but finds it difficult to apply all of Bill's advice.

Charlie does not understand the pretence surrounding celebrity and the interest that people have in it. He feels that stars giving interviews is all a big lie, but he is not sure who is lying.

He remembers his Aunt Helen babysitting and letting them stay up late to watch television.

He remembers the final episode of M*A*S*H and how his father went into the kitchen to secretly cry.

Charlie knows that a lot of kids at his school hate their parents. While he does not understand his parents, and feels sorry for them sometimes, he loves them very much.

Questions

1. How is Charlie getting on in school?

2. How does Charlie feel about movie stars that are terrible to watch?

3. What memory does he share about his Aunt Helen?

4. Why did his father go and make a sandwich during the final episode of M*A*S*H?
   What does this reveal about Charlie's father?
   What does this reveal about the world these characters live in?

5. How does Charlie feel about his parents?

6. Describe Charlie's personality and character, based on what you have read so far.

Letter Seven (October 6, 1991)

Summary

Charlie goes to a high school football game on his own and hangs around. He sees Nothing from shop class and introduces himself.

Nothing is called Patrick and he and Sam, the pretty girl he is with, are friendly to Charlie.

After the game, he goes to the Big Boy with them. They chat and ask him questions. He is glad to hear that they are stepbrother and stepsister and not a couple, as he would like to ask Sam out on a date someday.

That night Charlie has a sex dream about Sam. He feels ashamed about seeing Sam naked without her permission.

He considers telling Sam about it, and hopes it will not stop her from being a friend, because he really wants a friend again.

Questions

1. What is Charlie doing at the football game?
   What is your response to this?

2. Why does Charlie feel that he can approach Nothing at the football game?

3. How do Patrick and Sam treat Charlie?

4. What are Charlie's first impressions of Sam?

5. What is the relationship between Patrick and Sam?

6. What dream does Charlie have that night?
   Why is he ashamed?
   What is your response to this?

7. Do you consider Charlie to be an isolated character? Explain your point of view.

Letter Eight (October 14, 1991)

Summary

Charlie makes a joke about masturbation, to make his reader smile.

He tells Sam about the dream he had where she was naked. He cries and she is nice to him, telling him it is okay that he dreamt about her. She tells him that he is too young for her and not to waste his time thinking about her.

Patrick gives Charlie some advice about girls, saying that girls like guys to be a challenge.

Charlie watches couples in the hallways.

Bill sees him looking at people and asks him if he always thinks so much. Bill suggests that sometimes people use thought to avoid participating in life.

Charlie tells Bill about the boy hitting his sister. When he gets home, his parents are talking to his sister about it. She is not allowed see the boy anymore and is very upset about it.

She tells Charlie that she hates him and calls him a freak.

Charlie informs his reader that his father never hit them, apart from the time he hit Charlie for making Aunt Helen cry. He says his father is just stern sometimes.

Questions

1. Why does Charlie mention masturbation at the start of this letter?
   Is he a funny character, do you think?

2. What does Charlie tell Sam?
   Does anything about this surprise you?

3. How does Sam treat Charlie here?

4. What advice does Patrick give Charlie about girls?
   Is this good advice, in your view?

5. What does Charlie's teacher, Bill, talk to him about?
   What is your response to this?

6. Was Charlie right to tell Bill about the boy hitting his sister?

7. Bill tells Charlie that we accept the love we think we deserve.
   What does this mean?
   Do you think this is true?

8. What is going on when Charlie gets home from school?
   What is your response to this?
   Do Charlie's parents handle the situation well, do you think?

9. How does Charlie's sister treat him here?
   Is this fair?

Do you feel sorry for any of the characters here? Explain your view.

10. What view do you have of Charlie's father, based on the information you learn about him in this chapter?

Letter Nine (October 15, 1991)

Summary

Charlie masturbates a lot and feels guilty about it. He hopes he has not let God down.

Charlie's father speaks to the parents of the boy who hit Charlie's sister. He is non-confrontational. Keeping the boy away from Charlie's sister is the important thing, in his view.

Charlie asks his dad whether the boy has problems at home, but his dad is not interested in whether he does or not.

Questions

1. What is Charlie feeling guilty about?
   Why, do you think, has he included this in the letter?

2. Does his father handle the situation with the boy's parents well?
   What is the only important thing, as far as he is concerned?
   Do you agree with him?

3. Is Charlie's father too stern, in your view?

4. Charlie's dad says Charlie did the right thing, telling about the boy.
   Do you agree with him?
   Was there anything Charlie could have done differently?

5. If Charlie did the right thing, why is his sister mad at him?

6. What insight into Charlie's family dynamic have you gained so far?
   Include examples in your answer.

Letter Ten (October 28, 1991)

Summary

Charlie is trying to participate more, as his teacher, Bill, suggested.

He goes to the homecoming football game and pretends to Sam and Patrick that he is home from college for the occasion. Charlie likes that they do not think he is crazy for pretending to do things like this.

Sam invites him to a party after the game. He remembers a party of his brother's when he was a kid, where a couple asked to use the room he was in.

Despite the girl's protests and tears, she performed oral sex on the boy. They did other things, and she kept saying no. Charlie did not look as he felt sick.

When he tells Sam and Patrick about this incident, they go very quiet.

Charlie realises that the girl was raped and asks Sam if they should tell somebody, but she explains how difficult it would be to prove.

Charlie feels really good, driving to the party with Sam and Patrick after the game.
Everyone is friendly to him at the party. He eats a brownie and starts to feel

strange. Sam is annoyed with Bob for giving Charlie the brownie and they go to the kitchen to get Charlie a milkshake.

On his way back from the bathroom, Charlie sees Patrick kissing Brad, the quarterback. Brad is very anxious because Charlie has seen them together. Charlie promises that he will not tell anyone.

Back downstairs, they all toast Charlie and he starts to cry.

Charlie goes to the homecoming dance. The best part is letting the air out of Dave's tyres (Dave is the boy who raped the girl at the party).

Patrick and Brad do not speak at the dance, as Brad is with his girlfriend.

Charlie's sister dances with the boy she is not supposed to see anymore.

Patrick drives after the dance. As they go through the Fort Pitt Tunnel, Sam stands in the back of the pick-up and they listen to a beautiful song.

As they arrive downtown, the three of them are laughing and Charlie feels infinite.

Questions

1. Why hasn't Charlie written in a couple of weeks?

2. Did he like *Peter Pan*?

3. What is Charlie doing to try to participate more in things?

4. What does Charlie pretend at the homecoming game?

5. Is Charlie getting on well with Patrick and Sam?
   Use examples to support your point of view.

6. Charlie remembers a house party and a couple that wanted to "use the room" he was in.
   What is your reaction to this incident?

7. How do Sam and Patrick react when he tells them about this incident with the couple at the party?
   Can you explain their response?

8. What does Charlie realise about the party?
   What effect does this have on him?

9. What makes Charlie say that he feels infinite?

10. Describe the party they go to.

11. What effect does the brownie have on Charlie?

12. Why is Sam annoyed with Bob?

13. What does Charlie see on his way back from the bathroom?
    What does Charlie promise Patrick?

14. Why, do you think, is Patrick smiling so much when he comes downstairs?

15. What does Patrick mean when he calls Charlie a wallflower?

16. What was the best part of the homecoming dance?
    What does this tell you about Charlie?

17. What stops Brad from speaking to Patrick at the dance?
    What is your response to this?

18. Are you surprised that Charlie's sister dances with the boy she is forbidden from seeing?

19. What does Sam do as they approach the Fort Pitt Tunnel?

20. Are Sam and Patrick fun to be around?

21. Are Sam and Patrick good friends to Charlie, do you think?

22. "And in that moment, I swear we were infinite"
    Is Charlie an optimistic character, do you think?

23. What is the mood like at this point in the story?

24. How have things changed for Charlie since the story began?

Letter Eleven (November 7, 1991)

Summary

Charlie is having a good day. One of the girls from the party, Mary Elizabeth, explained Zen to him, and he thinks that Zen is a day like this.

Charlie tells us about Patrick and Brad. They had been fooling around at parties for months. Each time, Brad always insisted afterwards that he was wasted at the time.

Brad had sex with Patrick at a party in Sam and Patrick's and cried afterwards.

Patrick told him to pretend he was passed out, and went back to the party, asking the others if they had seen Brad.

Patrick was very worried about Brad, so he called Brad's parents to take him home.

Brad's parents sent him to rehabilitation and until a month ago, he avoided Patrick a lot.

Now, they meet up secretly. Patrick is glad that now Brad does not have to be drunk or stoned to make love.

Questions

1. What sort of day is it for Charlie?

2. Who is Mary Elizabeth?

3. What sort of relationship do Patrick and Brad have?

4. Why was Brad getting stoned or drunk before school?
   What is your response to this?

5. Why, do you think, did Brad cry after having sex with Patrick?
   What is your response to this?

6. Patrick and Brad keep their relationship totally secret. What does this suggest about the world they live in? How does this make you feel?

7. Does Patrick care about Brad, do you think?
   Use examples to support your view.

8. Do you think that Brad cares about Patrick?
   What makes their relationship difficult for him?
   What is your response to this?

9. What are your impressions of the world of this novel?
   Are characters free or restricted?
   What characterises how teenagers spend their time here?

Letter Twelve (November 8, 1991)

Summary

Charlie wants to be a writer when he grows up. He has been helping out on a fanzine called *Punk Rocky*, that Mary Elizabeth is in charge of.

Charlie really enjoyed going to *The Rocky Horror Picture Show* with Patrick and Sam. He loves Sam, who is now going out with a boy called Craig.

Craig plays Rocky in the show. He is "cut and hunky", and is very creative. Charlie wishes Sam would stop liking him, not because he is jealous, but because Craig does not listen to Sam properly.

Charlie's sister says Sam has low self-esteem. Once Charlie promised not to tell anyone, she talked to him about the boy she is not allowed to see anymore. They have been meeting secretly and plan to get married after college.

Charlie likes talking to his sister and is surprised that she told him so much.

Questions

1. What has Charlie decided he wants to do when he grows up?
   Why does he think this may be difficult?
   Would this career suit him, in your view?

2. What makes Mary Elizabeth an interesting person?

3. What are your impressions of Mary Elizabeth?

4. What does Charlie like about *The Rocky Horror Picture Show*?

5. Charlie says that he loves Sam.
   Does he really love her, in your opinion?

6. Describe Craig, Sam's new boyfriend.

7. Why does Charlie want Sam to stop liking Craig?
   What does this tell you about Charlie?
   What does it tell you about Sam?

8. What does Charlie's sister tell him about Sam?

9. What is going on with Charlie's sister and the boy she is not supposed to see?
   Does this surprise you?

10. Does Charlie like his sister?
    Do they have a good relationship?

Letter Thirteen (November 12, 1991)

Summary

Charlie talks about a science experiment where a rat or mouse will endure more pain for pleasure than for food. He finds this interesting.

Questions

1. Describe the experiment Charlie talks about.

2. What lesson does it reveal?
   Are you surprised by this?

3. Do you find this experiment interesting? Why/why not?

Letter Fourteen (November 15, 1991)

Summary

Charlie's brother has not called home in a number of weeks. When he does call, he talks more about the football team than his classes.

Charlie always wanted to be on a sports team so that he could have "glory days".

He was good at sport when he was little, but it used to make him too aggressive, so the doctors told his mom he would have to stop.

Charlie thinks that people in old photographs look happy, rugged and young.

He likes a story his dad tells about winning the state championship for baseball when he was in high school.

When watching football, Charlie sometimes thinks that these are the glory days for the player involved in a great touchdown.

Questions

1. Do Charlie's family miss his brother?

2. What does his brother talk about, when he calls home?

3. Does Charlie like sport?
   Why doesn't he play sport?
   What is your reaction to this?
   Is there a lot about Charlie that we do not know?

4. Do you think what Charlie says about old photographs is true?

5. What story of his dad's does Charlie like?
   Why does he like this story?

6. Is Charlie a deep thinker?
   Use examples to support your point of view.

7. Does this letter give you any insight into the life Charlie's parents have had?
   Use examples to support your answer.

Letter Fifteen (November 18, 1991)

Summary

Charlie's mom is upset because his brother will not be home for Thanksgiving. She takes Charlie clothes shopping and worries out loud about his brother and sister.

Sam and Patrick accept Charlie's invitation to dinner after the holidays. He is excited, as he has not had a friend to dinner since Michael came over last year.

When Michael stayed over they walked around the neighbourhood at night. Michael looked into all the windows and wondered if the people who lived in each house were nice.

Questions

1. Why does Charlie's mom take him clothes shopping?

2. Why is Charlie excited that Sam and Patrick will come to dinner?
   What is your response to this?

3. Michael figured out that the Tanners were getting a divorce.
   How did he know this, do you think?

4. How does mentioning Michael affect the mood of the story?

Letter Sixteen (November 23, 1991)

Summary

Charlie enjoys spending holidays with his mother's family and the predictable, familiar arguments his grandfather always starts.

Charlie's dad stays very quiet and drinks a lot on these occasions. He dislikes Charlie's grandfather, but keeps quiet about it.

One time, Charlie went with his brother when he drove Charlie's grandfather back to his retirement home. His grandfather talked about how hard his youth was. He mentioned an occasion when he beat his daughters for poor grades in school.

The whole family watch a video of Charlie's brother's football game. They are very proud of him.

As the others smile, Charlie notices that his grandfather is crying. He wonders whether it is better to let your kids be happy and not go to college, or to make sure that they have a better life than you.

After the game, everyone says what they are thankful for. Charlie says he is thankful for the game on television, because nobody fought. His statement makes the others uncomfortable.

He hugs and kisses his grandfather before he leaves, even though his grandfather does not appreciate it or want him to.

Questions

1. Why does Charlie enjoy holidays with his extended family?

2. In what way are the fights always the same?
   Who is responsible for these fights?
   Would you like to attend a family gathering like this?

3. Why do Charlie's cousins go to the bathroom out in the bushes?

4. What does Charlie's dad do at these family events?
   Can you explain his behaviour here?

5. What did Charlie learn about his grandfather on the drive back to his retirement home one time?
   What is your response to this?

6. What did Charlie's grandfather do when Helen and Charlie's mom got poor grades?
   Comment on this.

7. How do the whole family react to watching Charlie's brother's football game?

8. Why does Charlie's grandfather cry?

9. Do you think it is better to have happy kids who don't go to college, or that it is better to make sure your kids have a better life than you, even if your relationship

suffers because of it?
Give reasons for your answer.

10. How does Charlie make the others uncomfortable?

11. Why does Charlie kiss his grandfather?
What does this tell you about Charlie?

12. How does his grandfather's reaction make you feel?

13. What do you learn about Charlie's family from reading this letter?

Letter Seventeen (December 7, 1991)

Summary

Charlie gets Patrick in the "Secret Santa" that Sam's friends are doing. He makes him a mix tape, and puts a lot of thought into it.

Charlie thinks about how much people have loved the songs on the tape and how this music has helped people.

He is still reading extra books for Bill. They are all his favourites.

Questions

1. What is "Secret Santa"?

2. Why is Charlie glad that he got Patrick?
   Why hasn't he seen much of Patrick lately?

3. What present has he got for Patrick?
   Is this a thoughtful gift?
   Explain your point of view.

4. What did Charlie think about when he finally held the tape in his hand?
   What does this tell you about him?

5. Is Charlie enjoying his extra reading?

Letter Eighteen (December 11, 1991)

Summary

Patrick loves the tape that Charlie made him.

Charlie plans to give him magnetic poetry next.

He is disappointed with his own gift of socks, and suspects that Mary Elizabeth is his Secret Santa.

Questions

1. Why does Charlie think that Patrick knows he is his Secret Santa?

2. What will Patrick's second gift be?

3. What gift does Charlie receive?
Is he happy with this?
Would you be, in his position?

Letter Nineteen (December 19, 1991)

Summary

Charlie receives slacks, a tie, a white shirt, shoes and an old belt from his Secret Santa. He is instructed to wear everything to the party.

He gives Patrick watercolours and a harmonica for gifts three and four. He will give him *The Mayor of Castro Street*, a book about Harvey Milk, as his final gift.

Charlie is too busy to write about the finals he has taken.

Questions

1. What gifts and instructions does Charlie receive?

2. What gifts does he give Patrick?
   Are these good presents, do you think?

3. What is Charlie's final gift for Patrick?
   Is this a good present, do you think?

4. Why hasn't Charlie written about his finals and school?
   Is this a good or bad thing, in your view?

Letter Twenty (December 21, 1991)

Summary

Charlie feels very welcome at the party in Sam and Patrick's, their parents are nice and friendly. After dinner, their parents leave them to their party in the games room.

Charlie has made a copy of a poem for Patrick as his last gift. He reads it aloud and everyone is quiet afterwards.

Patrick gives Charlie a suit coat to complete his outfit. Charlie thinks he looks good.

Charlie gives thoughtful gifts to each of the others too. He gives Sam the Beatles' record, "Something" and a card.

She hugs him and whispers that she loves him. She gives Charlie a typewriter.

Sam asks Charlie if he has ever kissed a girl. She wants the first person he kisses to love him, so she kisses him.

Charlie includes the poem he read for Patrick about suicide (The poem is 'A Person/A Paper/A Promise by Dr Earl Reum, although Charlie does not state this.)

Questions

1. What is Sam and Patrick's house like?

2. What does Charlie think of Sam and Patrick's parents?

3. What is Patrick's final gift from Charlie?
   What effect does it have on the group?

4. What gifts does Charlie give the other party guests?
   Does this tell you anything about Charlie?
   How does Sam respond to Charlie's gift?

5. What present does Sam give Charlie?
   Is this a good gift for him, do you think?

6. Why does Sam kiss Charlie?
   What is the mood like at this moment?
   Do you think that Charlie and Sam will go out together?

7. What is the poem that Charlie reads for Patrick about?
   How does it make you feel?

8. Does Charlie have a good time at the party?

9. Describe Charlie, now that you have got to know him.

10. Are Patrick and Sam good friends to Charlie?
    Give reasons for your answer.

11. Is Charlie happier now that he is friends with Sam and Patrick, in your view?
    Refer to the text to support your response.

12. Is having friends important to most teenagers, do you think?
    Give reasons for your answer.

Letter Twenty-One (December 23, 1991)

Summary

Charlie spends the day walking around the neighbourhood, watching kids sled.

He is glad that Christmas and his birthday will soon be over. He feels himself going to the bad place he used to go to, when his aunt Helen was gone. When this happens, things slip away and he sees nothing.

He plans to be busy over Christmas while Sam and Patrick are away.

Questions

1. How does Charlie spend the day?

2. Why is Charlie glad that Christmas and his birthday will soon be over?
   What is your response to this?

3. It seems that there is something Charlie is not telling us. What could this be?

4. How does Charlie describe the "bad place"?
   Does it sound frightening to you?

5. What stopped Charlie from going to the bad place this morning?
   What is your response to this?

6. What plans does Charlie have while Patrick and Sam are gone?
   Is he looking forward to the next few days at all, do you think?

7. What would make Charlie feel much better on his birthday?
   Does he depend on Sam and Patrick a lot, do you think?

Letter Twenty-Two (December 25, 1991)

Summary

Charlie is in his dad's old bedroom. He does not feel very well and is starting to get scared. He is thinking too fast.

The day before this, Charlie feels weird because he does not know what present to buy his dad. He feels sad because he does not know him.

Charlie's dad and brother are very late getting back from the airport. This annoys Charlie's sister because she wants to go and buy a present for her secret boyfriend.

Charlie goes to his room, followed by his mom. She knows something is wrong. She guesses it is to do with aunt Helen and does not let him talk about it and get upset.

He calms down enough to go downstairs and put up luminaria. He distracts himself by reading and thinking about driving for the rest of the evening.

On the drive on Christmas day, Charlie's brother talks about meeting his girlfriend and bickers with Charlie's sister. Charlie's brother says that his girlfriend would not let a man hit her.

To stop their arguing, Charlie's dad slams on the brakes and stares at them. They apologise to one another.

Charlie's dad gets in the back with Charlie's brother and sister and lets Charlie drive the rest of the way.

They have dinner at Charlie's grandma's. He thinks about her second husband beating her and her children for seven years. When her brother, uncle Phil, found out, he and his friends beat the guy up so badly that he died in hospital four days later.

Charlie's aunt Rebecca had the same kind of husbands. Charlie gets sad when he wonders how her three children will turn out.

His dad's room is much as he left it. Charlie understands why his dad had to leave this house, so that he could have a life of his own. His dad feels guilty though, for leaving his mother and sister.

Questions

1. How is Charlie feeling as this letter begins?

2. What made Charlie feel weird when he went present shopping with his mom and sister?

3. What does he get for his dad in the end?

4. Why is Charlie's sister in such a bad mood?

5. Why is Charlie so sad?
   Why doesn't his mom let him talk about it?
   Does she know Charlie well?
   Is not talking about something that upsets you a good strategy, in your view?

6. What are 'luminaria'?
   Does this sound like a nice tradition? Why/why not?

7. How does Charlie distract himself from thinking about his birthday?

8. What insight into Charlie's family life does the drive to Ohio give you?

9. How did Charlie's brother meet his girlfriend?

10. Do Charlie's brother and sister get on well?
    Use examples to support your view.

11. Is there truth in his sister's statements about how women look and her comments about sororities and fraternities? Do the rest of the family listen to her views? Why is this, do you think?

12. Describe Charlie's grandma.

13. What is Charlie's first memory? Does it sound funny to you?

14. What happened to Charlie's grandma's second husband? What is your reaction to this?

15. Why, do you think, does Charlie's great uncle Phil love to tell this story? What is your response to this?

16. What makes Charlie sad when he thinks about Aunt Rebecca's children?

17. Describe Charlie's dad's old room.

18. Why did Charlie's dad have to leave this house?

19. Does Charlie's dad have a good relationship with his family?

20. What is the mood like as this letter ends?

21. What insight into life does learning about Charlie's dad's upbringing give you?

22. Does this letter give you a positive or negative impression of life?

Give reasons for your answer.

Letter Twenty-Three (December 26, 1991)

Summary

Charlie's family usually visit Aunt Helen's grave on the drive home. Every time they visit her grave, Charlie and his mom like to talk about something really great about her.

Charlie is unsure whether he should write about the bad thing that happened to his Aunt Helen. Nobody in the family ever talks about it.

Helen was molested by a friend of the family. She finally told her dad about it, but he did not believe her. Her mother never said anything either. The man kept coming over for visits.

Helen drank and took drugs a lot. She had problems with men and was a very unhappy person, in and out of hospitals all the time.

She moved in with Charlie's family and started sorting her life out. Like Charlie's immediate family, she always got him a separate birthday present.

Helen died in a car accident on Christmas Eve 1983. At first, seven year old Charlie did not believe this news, he thought there had been some mistake.

Charlie was sent to see a doctor who asked him questions. He was not allowed go to his aunt's funeral. He is not sure how long he kept seeing the doctor, or how long he was kept out of school for, but it was a long time.

The last thing his Aunt Helen told him before she died, was that she was going to buy his birthday present.

Charlie blames himself for her being in a car crash that day.

Questions

1. What do Charlie's family usually do on the way home?

2. What do Charlie and his mom want Aunt Helen to know?

3. Charlie is unsure whether he should write about the bad thing that happened to Aunt Helen.
   Why is this the case, do you think?

4. What bad thing happened to Aunt Helen?
   How did her father react when she told him?
   What is your response to this?

5. What sort of life did Helen have?
   What sort of person do you imagine her to be?

6. Why did Helen move in with Charlie's family?

7. Did Charlie have a good relationship with his Aunt Helen, do you think?

8. What happened on December 24, 1983?
   How does this development make you feel?

9. Why didn't Charlie cry when he heard the news?

10. Why wasn't Charlie allowed to attend her funeral?

11. Why does Charlie blame himself for his aunt's death?
    Do you understand why he feels this way?
    Do you feel sorry for Charlie here?

12. Does learning about Aunt Helen's death help to explain Charlie's recent behaviour?

13. How does knowing about the 'bad thing' that happened Aunt Helen and the story of her death contribute to the mood here?

14. Neither of Helen's parents did anything about her being molested.
    What does this tell you about the world of this novel?
    What does their inaction tell you about people and life?
    How does their behaviour here make you feel?

15. What makes this letter sad?
    Be precise in your answer.

Letter Twenty-Four (December 30, 1991)

Summary

Charlie drives to his aunt Helen's grave and tells her about his life. He promises only to cry about important things.

He distracts himself from crying by re-reading *The Catcher in the Rye*. He wants to stop thinking and fears he might have to go back to the doctor.

Questions

1. Why won't Charlie see Sam and Patrick when they come home tonight?

2. Why does Charlie drive to see his aunt Helen?

3. What has Charlie been doing to stop himself from crying?
   Does he cry a lot?
   Why is this, do you think?

4. Why does Charlie not want to think?

5. Charlie is afraid that he might have to go back to the doctor.
   Do you think this is likely?

6. Are you worried about Charlie's mental health?
   Give reasons for your answer.

7. Does Charlie have a lot of emotional problems?

8. Does he have a lot of support from friends and family?
   Use examples to support your view.

Letter Twenty-Five (January 1, 1992)

Summary

It is four a.m. Charlie cannot sleep.

He drove to the Big Boy and saw Sam and Patrick with Craig and Brad. He was very sad because he wanted to be alone with them.

Charlie's letter is disjointed, he appears to have taken drugs at the party.

He started shovelling Bob's driveway during the party when he remembered the good day he had when he mowed his lawn.

Mark, a kid at the party, looks at the stars with Charlie, saying they are in a black glass dome and the stars are holes. He says when you go to heaven, it breaks open, into white light. Charlie sees this and feels small.

Charlie is aware of others reading the books he has read and listening to the songs he listens to.

He writes that he does not really know what he is saying, he is seeing things move.

He can hear Sam and Craig having sex. He understands the end of the poem.

Questions

1. Why is Charlie awake at four o'clock in the morning?

2. What made Charlie very sad at the Big Boy?
   How do you respond to this?

3. What made Charlie shovel Bob's driveway at the party?

4. Does this letter make sense to you?
   Include examples in your answer.
   What is going on here?

5. What does Charlie mean when he says, "this all feels very familiar"?
   What is he describing here?

6. What can Charlie hear?
   What effect is this having on him?

7. Describe the mood at this point.

Letter Twenty-Six (January 4, 1992)

Summary

Charlie apologises for the last letter.

He spent the night of the party looking for an envelope and stamp to mail the letter. When he posted it, he started to throw up.

Thoughts ran through his mind and the trees kept moving, so he lay down and made a snow angel.

A policeman found him asleep in the snow and took him to the emergency room.

Charlie used to wander off and fall asleep when he was seeing the doctors, so no-one gets in trouble.

The doctor suggests that Charlie should see a psychiatrist again. All Charlie can think about is that they missed his brother's football game because of him.

His family are all nice to him when he gets home. His sister helps him fix his hair, which he has cut chunks out of.

He decides never to take LSD again.

Questions

1. How did Charlie spend the rest of the night at the party? What does this suggest about the condition he was in?

2. Why does he lie down to make a snow angel?

3. Why is he taken to the emergency room?

4. Why does nobody get in trouble?

5. What stops Charlie from telling the truth?

6. How do Charlie's family treat him when he gets home? Why do they treat him this way?

7. What happened Charlie's hair?

8. Do Charlie's family know he took LSD?
Do you find this funny or sad?
Comment on Charlie's drug use. Are you surprised to learn he took LSD?

9. Do you think that Charlie's family are worried about him? Give reasons for your answer.

10. Based on what you have read so far, do Charlie's family communicate well with each other? Give reasons for your answer.

Letter Twenty-Seven (January 14, 1992)

Summary

Charlie feels like a faker, secretly putting his life back together. He finds it difficult to read or talk to his brother on the phone.

He gets a library book to find out about LSD. He is very worried about the effect it will have on him.

He is teased constantly for wearing his new suit to school.

He goes outside to smoke with Patrick and Sam and tells them what is wrong. Sam talks to him and helps him focus on what looks normal.

Charlie is very relieved.

Bill is very happy with his latest paper.

Questions

1. Why does Charlie feel like a faker?

2. Why is Charlie worried about the LSD?

3. How does Charlie find out about LSD? How would you find out about something that was worrying you in the present day?

4. Why is Charlie having such a bad day?

5. How does Sam help Charlie here? Is she a good friend?

6. How is Charlie getting on in advanced english? Are you surprised that he is successful in this class while struggling with personal problems? What does this tell you about life?

7. "I'm now up to about ten cigarettes a day." How has Charlie changed since the novel began? Can you explain the changes in his behaviour?

8. Does Charlie's LSD episode tell you anything about the world of this story?

Letter Twenty-Eight (January 25, 1992)

Summary

Charlie is having a good week. He likes his new psychiatrist. They talk about what he feels, thinks and remembers. The best thing about the psychiatrist is that he has music magazines in his waiting room.

Charlie reads a piece about Nirvana that he and his friends discuss after *Rocky Horror* at the Big Boy.

He really enjoys participating in the discussion, knowing that all over the world, people are having similar conversations.

Questions

1. How is Charlie feeling now?

2. What is Charlie's psychiatrist like?

3. Why have Charlie's parents sent him to see a psychiatrist, do you think?

4. Why was Charlie happy to make his mom smile?
   How does this make you feel?

5. Charlie is scared by the idea of being wrongly punished for something.
   Is this a common fear, in your view?

6. What do Charlie and his friends discuss at the Big Boy?

7. Is Charlie having a good time?

8. How important is music in teenagers' lives?
   Give reasons for you answer.

Letter Twenty-Nine (February 2, 1992)

Summary

Charlie visits Bill in his office after school to discuss *On The Road*. Bill lets him smoke in his office.

They chat about Charlie's life and he asks Bill some questions about his.

Charlie's latest book, *Naked Lunch*, makes no sense to him, so he goes from family member to family member, annoying each of them in turn, before returning to his reading.

Questions

1. What do Charlie and Bill talk about?
   Does Charlie have a good relationship with his teacher?
   Is this a regular teacher-student relationship?
   Explain your view.

2. What is Bill like, based on what you have read so far?

3. What different things does Charlie do, rather than read *Naked Lunch*?

4. Why does he give up on watching television with his sister?

5. Why does he stop helping his mother in the kitchen?

6. Why does he stop watching hockey with his father?

7. Does this letter add anything to your understanding of Charlie's personality?

Letter Thirty (February 8, 1992)

Summary

Mary Elizabeth has asked Charlie to the Sadie Hawkins' dance. She is very happy with the latest edition of *Punk Rocky*. Each of the group of friends contributed to it.

Craig does not turn up to play Rocky in *The Rocky Horror Picture Show*. Mary Elizabeth asks Charlie if he can play Rocky. He is anxious about getting an erection wearing only a bathing suit. Then Sam asks Charlie to play Rocky, so he does. He really enjoys it.

After the show, Mary Elizabeth asks Charlie to the dance.

Charlie asks his sister for advice for his date, but she is distracted and does not answer him.

Questions

1. Who is Charlie's date?

2. Why is the latest issue of *Punk Rocky* so good, according to Mary Elizabeth?

3. Does it sound like a good magazine to you?

4. Why does Patrick want his nude photograph in the magazine?

5. Why does Charlie have to play Rocky in the show?
   Why is he anxious about playing Rocky?
   What convinces him to do it?
   Would you stand in like this, in his position?

6. Does Charlie enjoy being in the show?

7. Does Charlie really care about Sam? Explain your view.

8. Why does Charlie ask his sister for advice?

9. How is Charlie's sister behaving lately?
   What is going on with her, do you think?

Letter Thirty-One (February 9, 1992)

Summary

Charlie knows that Sam would never ask him to the dance, but he wants her to be jealous that Mary Elizabeth has.

Sam is not jealous at all though, and gives him advice for the date.

Questions

1. Does Charlie like Mary Elizabeth?

2. What reaction does Charlie want Sam to have about Mary Elizabeth asking him to the dance?
   Do you understand why Charlie wants her to feel this way?

3. What advice does Sam give Charlie?
   Does this sound like good advice to you?

4. Do you think taking Mary Elizabeth to the dance is a good idea, when Charlie is more interested in Sam?
   Give reasons for your answer.

Letter Thirty-Two (February 15, 1992)

Summary

Mary Elizabeth talks about herself a lot at the dance. Charlie learns a lot about her.

He does not kiss her goodnight, but says that he would like to go out again sometime.

Sam takes Patrick to the dance, as Craig does not want to go.

Charlie's sister has a huge fight with her boyfriend during a slow song and rushes off to the bathroom.

When Charlie gets home, he finds his sister crying in the basement. He tries to talk to her, but she wants to be left alone. When he turns to go, she hugs him fiercely and tells him that she is pregnant.

When she told her boyfriend at the dance, he said the baby was not his and broke up with her.

She plans to go to a clinic for a termination on Saturday and needs Charlie to go with her.

Questions

1. What are your impressions of Mary Elizabeth after reading about the dance?
   Would you like to spend more time with her?

2. Would you go out with her again, if you were Charlie?

3. Why does Sam bring Patrick to the dance?

4. What happens between Charlie's sister and her boyfriend at the dance?
   Are you surprised to hear this?

5. What state is Charlie's sister in after the dance?
   Why is she so upset?

6. Are you surprised to learn that she is pregnant?

7. What is her boyfriend's reaction to the pregnancy?
   What is your response to this?
   Does his reaction surprise you?

8. What does Charlie's sister plan to do next?
   How will Charlie help her?

9. Do you feel sorry for Charlie's sister?

10. What does Charlie's sister's boyfriend's reaction to the pregnancy tell you about the world of this novel?

Letter Thirty-Three (February 23, 1992)

Summary

Charlie cannot concentrate on his new book in the clinic waiting room. He tries to read some magazines, but finds himself thinking about the way the women in the magazines are treated in real life.

He thinks about his sister and wonders how she will look when she comes out. He starts crying and goes outside.

When his sister finds him in the car, she is furious that he is smoking. This reassures Charlie that she will not be changed too much by terminating the pregnancy.

She sleeps in the car and Charlie reads until it gets dark. They go home and tell their parents they went to a movie and McDonald's and that Charlie's sister taught him to drive on highways.

That night his sister tells Charlie to keep the termination a secret, as she plans to tell her old boyfriend that the pregnancy was a false alarm.

She asks him to stop smoking because she loves him. He tells her that he loves her too.

Questions

1. What does Charlie think about in the waiting room of the clinic?

2. "That's when I started thinking about my sister."
   Does Charlie know and understand his sister well?
   Do they have a good relationship?

3. Why does Charlie start to cry?

4. How does his sister react when she finds him?
   How does this make him feel?

5. What makes Charlie's sister start to laugh?

6. Why don't they go home right away?

7. What story do they tell their parents to explain where they were all day?
   Are you surprised that their parents believe them?

8. Why does Charlie's sister ask him to keep the termination a secret?
   What is your response to this?

9. What is your view of Charlie's sister's relationship with her secret boyfriend?
   Do you think they will get back together?

10. What is your response to Charlie calling the 1-800 number and wishing Michelle a good night?

11.	Charlie's sister does not want anyone to know about the termination.
	If they were to know, what reaction do you think her parents would have?
	Would they be sympathetic?

12.	What insight into the treatment of women in society does this letter give you?

Letter Thirty-Four (March 7, 1992)

Summary

Charlie asks to borrow his father's car as Mary Elizabeth has asked him out again.

Charlie's dad talks to him about sex. He tells him to use protection, and to take no as an answer.

Charlie and Mary Elizabeth go to see an art movie. Charlie does not think it is very good, but Mary Elizabeth enjoys it and calls it an "articulate" film.

Afterwards they go to an underground record store and Mary Elizabeth gives Charlie a tour. She buys him a record by Billie Holiday and invites him to her house to listen to it.

They drink brandy and listen to the record in her basement. Mary Elizabeth sits on his lap, facing him, and starts kissing him.

Later, she asks him if he thinks she is pretty. He tells her that she is very pretty.

Questions

1. Mary Elizabeth has asked Charlie out again.
   Is she interested in him as a potential boyfriend, do you think?
   Is he interested in her?

2. What advice about sex does Charlie's dad give him?
   Is this good advice, do you think?

3. Where do Charlie and Mary Elizabeth go on their date?

4. Why does Mary Elizabeth love the underground record store?

5. What happens in Mary Elizabeth's basement?

6. Why is Charlie nervous?

7. Does Charlie really like Mary Elizabeth, do you think?

Letter Thirty-Five (March 28, 1992)

Summary

Mary Elizabeth has told the others about her and Charlie and now everything is different.

She calls him after school every day and talks about herself for ages, something he is not enjoying.

She invites herself along to the dinner at his house for Sam and Patrick and talks the whole time.

Charlie is disappointed that his parents do not get to know his friends as a result of this.

Charlie asks his sister for advice about Mary Elizabeth. She tells him that Mary Elizabeth is suffering from low self-esteem.

Charlie feels sad. He feels he does not really know who Mary Elizabeth is and does not want to be another thing that she is in charge of.

He calls his brother, but his roommate says that he is busy.

Questions

1. What is different about Charlie's paper on *Walden*?

2. How have things been different since that night with Mary Elizabeth?

3. Is Charlie happy to be going out with Mary Elizabeth?

4. Does he enjoy their phone conversations?
   Would you?

5. Why is Charlie disappointed by the dinner for Sam and Patrick?
   Do you understand how he feels?
   Is he being selfish here?

6. What view does Charlie have of "sex things" with Mary Elizabeth?

7. What advice does Charlie's sister give him about Mary Elizabeth?
   Does this sound like good advice to you?

8. Why is Charlie sad about Mary Elizabeth?
   Do you understand why he feels like this?

9. Why doesn't he talk to his brother about Mary Elizabeth?

10. What would you do about Mary Elizabeth if you were Charlie?

Letter Thirty-Six (April 18, 1992)

Summary

Mary Elizabeth gives Charlie a book of poetry by e.e. cummings and tells him to show it to everyone.

Although he acts grateful, he is not at all. After school, he returns the book to the bookstore, but feels terrible about it and starts crying. His sister drives him to get the book back.

That night on the phone, when she asks, he tells Mary Elizabeth that he got her something nice. Then he has to go and buy her something.

He gives her *To Kill A Mockingbird* and explains that it is special to him because it is the first book Bill gave him to read.

She thanks him, but says that she has already read it and that it is over-rated.

Charlie walks around after school until one in the morning.

His father tells him to act like a man.

The next day, Mary Elizabeth wonders where he was when she called. He lies that he was in the Big Boy, reading the book of poetry she gave him.

After *The Rocky Horror Picture Show* they go back to Craig's apartment and play truth or dare. Charlie chooses dare all night to avoid telling Mary Elizabeth the truth because of a game.

When Patrick dares Charlie to kiss the prettiest girl in the room, he kisses Sam, not Mary Elizabeth. He thinks that kissing Mary Elizabeth for the dare would be lying.

Mary Elizabeth goes to the bathroom with Sam and Patrick takes Charlie outside.

Charlie starts crying and Patrick takes him home, telling him to stay away for a while.

Charlie thinks that something is really wrong with him, but he does not know what it is.

Questions

1. What gift does Mary Elizabeth give to Charlie?
   Why isn't he grateful?
   Would you be grateful, if you were him?

2. What does Charlie do after school?

3. Why does he start crying?

4. How does his sister help Charlie?

5. What stops Charlie from being honest with Mary Elizabeth?

6. How does Mary Elizabeth respond to Charlie's gift of *To Kill a Mockingbird*?
   How would you feel if you were him?

7. Why does Charlie stay out until one in the morning?
   Does his father have sympathy for him?
   Do you?

8. What lie does Charlie tell Mary Elizabeth about where he was the day before?
   Do you think this lie could be problematic?

9. Charlie says he is getting as mad as he used to when playing sports.
   What, exactly, has him feeling this way?

10. Why does Charlie choose dare over truth all night at Craig's?

11. Why does Charlie kiss Sam?
    How do the others respond?

12. Was Charlie wrong to kiss Sam?

13. Was Charlie stupid to kiss Sam like this?

14. Do you think that Charlie kissing Sam like this is a big deal? Explain your point of view fully.

15. Why does Charlie start crying?

16. How is Charlie feeling as this letter ends?
    What is the mood like at this point?

17. Do you think that Charlie's actions here will cost him his group of friends?
    Explain your point of view fully.

Letter Thirty-Seven (April 26, 1992)

Summary

Charlie calls Mary Elizabeth and apologises.

Patrick calls him once, but otherwise, he hears nothing from his friends.

His sister has met a new boy.

His brother has broken up with his girlfriend.

Charlie is feeling very low. He says he has brought it all on himself and wishes that he were different.

He is smoking pot all the time.

Questions

1. What does Charlie say to Mary Elizabeth when he calls her?

2. What news does Charlie have about his family?

3. Is Charlie's brother interested in Charlie and how he is getting on, do you think?

4. How is Charlie feeling at present?

5. Why does Charlie call Bob?
   What is your response to this?

6. Charlie is feeling very alone at this point in the story. Is this his fault?
   Do you feel sorry for Charlie here?
   If you were Charlie, how would you deal with this situation?

Letter Thirty-Eight (April 29, 1992)

Summary

School is difficult for Charlie because he cannot go to the places he used to.

He thinks about the teachers and students, wondering about them and their lives.

Charlie has started going to the shopping mall, trying to figure out why people go there.

He sees a tough-looking kid help a small boy find his mom, and then follows the mom and child to the food places. He watches them, wondering about the mom's life.

He finds all the tired people out shopping to be very unsettling.

In school, he approaches Susan, even though her friends go quiet and she looks like she does not want to talk to him. He asks her if she ever misses Michael, but she does not answer him.

Questions

1. Why is it hard for Charlie at school?

2. Why has Charlie been going to the shopping mall?

3. Does anything about the incident with the lost boy strike you as interesting?

4. Why does Charlie find watching the people in the food places unsettling?
   Does this tell you anything about Charlie?

5. How does Susan react when she sees Charlie?
   How do her friends react?
   What is going on here?

6. Why does Charlie speak to Susan?
   How does she respond?
   Why does she respond like this?
   How would you feel, if you were Charlie?

7. How is Charlie doing these days, in your view?

8. What is the mood like, at this point in the story?

Letter Thirty-Nine (May 2, 1992)

Summary

Charlie goes to buy more pot from Bob. He hears that Brad's father caught Patrick and Brad together and beat Brad up. Brad has not been back to school.

Charlie does not know whether he should call Patrick or not. He goes to *The Rocky Horror Picture Show* to see him onstage and misses his friends. He pretends they are in the car with him as he drives home.

His sister is watching a movie with her new boyfriend, Erik. He tries to watch the end of it with them, but his sister says they want to be alone, so he leaves.

Questions

1. What is Bob like, based on this letter?

2. What news does Charlie hear from Bob?
   What is your reaction to this?
   What does Brad's father's behaviour here tell you about the society and world of this novel?

3. Why is Charlie reluctant to call Patrick?
   What would you do?

4. How does Charlie feel watching *The Rocky Horror Picture Show*?

5. What does Charlie pretend as he drives home?

6. What is Charlie's sister's new boyfriend like?

7. Why doesn't Charlie leave her and Erik alone to start with?

8. Are you worried about Charlie?
   Give reasons for your answer.

9. Are you glad that Charlie's sister has a new boyfriend? Why/why not?

Letter Forty (May 8, 1992)

Summary

Brad is back at school. He is very changed, lacking his former confidence. He ignores Patrick in school, even when Patrick gets upset while talking to him.

Charlie sees Patrick outside, smoking and crying, but does not approach him.

On Thursday, Patrick speaks to Brad at lunch, but is ignored. As he walks away, Brad yells "Faggot!" after him.

Patrick punches Brad and they fight. Brad's friends join in. Charlie cannot watch them hurt Patrick, so he gets involved.

Charlie badly hurts two of Brad's friends. He warns Brad not to hurt Patrick again.

Patrick and Brad's friends are suspended, while Charlie and Brad get a month's detention.

On the first day of detention, Brad thanks Charlie for stopping his friends from beating Patrick up.

Sam is waiting for him after detention and drives him home. She talks about Mary Elizabeth on the drive.

Charlie cries when she says they can be friends again. She tells him to apologise to Mary Elizabeth, which he does, and things are okay between them.

Patrick quits *The Rocky Horror Picture Show* and sits in the seats with Charlie. He is troubled and unhappy.

Questions

1. What is different about Brad when he comes back to school?
   Can you explain this change in him?

2. How is Brad treating Patrick?
   What do you think of this?

3. What effect is Brad's behaviour and attitude towards him having on Patrick?
   How does this make you feel?

4. Why does Brad yell "Faggot!" at Patrick?
   What is making him act like this?

5. Describe the fight.

6. What does Charlie do when the fight breaks out?
   Are you surprised that he does this?

7. How does Charlie threaten Brad?

8. What punishment are the boys given for fighting?
   Is this fair?

9. What does Brad say to Charlie on the first day of detention?
   Can you explain what is going on here?
   Do you feel sorry for Brad?
   Explain your point of view.

10. Are you surprised that Sam is waiting for Charlie after detention?
    What do Sam and Charlie talk about in the pickup truck?

11. How does Charlie react when Sam says they can be friends again?

12. Is Sam a good friend?
    How would you feel if you were Charlie?

13. How are things between Charlie and Mary Elizabeth at *The Rocky Horror Picture Show*?

14. Are you surprised that Mary Elizabeth has a new boyfriend?

15. What makes the evening tense?

16. How is Patrick?

17. Why do Charlie's friends accept him again after isolating him for so long?

18. Are things back the way they were?

19. What is the mood like as this chapter ends?

20. Do you think that Charlie has been treated badly by his group of friends or not?

21. If you were Charlie, would you be eager to re-connect with this group?
    Give reasons for your answer.

Letter Forty-One (May 11, 1992)

Summary

Patrick comes and picks Charlie up on Saturday morning. He has not showered or changed his clothes from the night before. He says everything will be different when he goes to college.

They spend the day together. Whenever Patrick gets tired, they get coffee and Patrick has another Mini Thin or two.

Patrick shows Charlie all the places where he used to meet Brad. They end up at the golf course, drinking red wine.

They tell each other stories about kids from school and laugh.

On the drive home, Patrick thanks Charlie for that day in the cafeteria.

They park on the driveway and Patrick kisses Charlie. Charlie lets him. Patrick cries and talks about Brad, and Charlie listens.

Questions

1. Describe Patrick when he comes to pick Charlie up.

2. Why is Patrick looking forward to college?

3. How do they spend the day?

4. What do they do when Patrick gets tired?

5. Why do they end up at the golf course?

6. What do the boys talk about at the golf course?

7. What happens when Patrick drops Charlie home?
   Can you explain what is going on here?
   Does Charlie surprise you here?
   Explain your point of view.

8. Is Patrick taking advantage of Charlie?
   Fully explain your point of view.

Letter Forty-Two (May 17, 1992)

Summary

Charlie is spending a lot of time with Patrick, who is hurting badly.

One night they go to a park where men go to find men anonymously. A sports presenter talks to Charlie, but walks away when Charlie asks what it is like to be on television.

Patrick takes him to lots of places to find men. Patrick is excited as every night begins, but is sad after picking up guys.

On this night, they go to the park again and Patrick sees Brad with some guy. After seeing this, Patrick drives Charlie home, and instead of kissing him, thanks him for being his friend.

Questions

1. How does Charlie feel every morning?

2. Why is Charlie spending so much time with Patrick?

3. Why does Patrick bring Charlie to the park?

4. Why does the sports presenter get up and walk away from Charlie?

5. Is Charlie a very naive character?
   Use examples to support the points you make.

6. How does Patrick feel on the nights when he picks someone up?
   How is Patrick doing, in your view?

7. Where do they see Brad?
   What does this mean?

8. How does Patrick react to seeing Brad like this?
   How would you feel, if you were Patrick?

9. Why can't Brad be open about his sexuality?
   What does this tell you about the society he is living in?

Letter Forty-Three (May 21, 1992)

Summary

School is nearly over. The seniors are getting ready for graduation and prom.

Charlie has watched some films for Bill and has been given his final novel.

If he catches up on his schoolwork he will finish the year with straight A's.

Patrick has stopped drinking since seeing Brad in the park. He wants to graduate and get to college.

Questions

1. What work has Charlie done for Bill lately?

2. Is Bill a good teacher, in your view?
   What makes a good teacher, in your opinion?

3. What are Charlie's grades like?
   Does this surprise you?

4. How did Charlie improve his math scores?
   Does this sound like good teaching and learning to you?

5. What makes Charlie think that Patrick is getting better?
   Do you agree with Charlie?

6. What does college represent for Patrick, in your opinion?

Letter Forty-Four (May 27, 1992)

Summary

Charlie is enjoying *The Fountainhead* and has begun writing a story of his own, but is stumped after the first sentence.

He has a lot of free time as everyone is busy with prom and graduation.

Charlie is looking forward to his own graduation and senior prom and hopes he will be a valedictorian.

Questions

1. What inspired Charlie to start writing a story?

2. Why has he had a lot of free time this past week?

3. Is Charlie looking forward to his graduation? What hopes does he have?

4. What is the mood like in this letter?

Letter Forty-Five (June 2, 1992)

Summary

Some seniors filled the pool with grape Kool-Aid as their senior prank.

Everybody is busy finishing up the school year. They have all figured out the schools that they will go to next.

Charlie enjoys *The Fountainhead*. He tells his psychiatrist all about it and his friends, but his psychiatrist keeps asking questions about when Charlie was younger. Charlie feels he is repeating himself to him.

Questions

1. What is the senior prank?

2. Why is it an exciting time?

3. Why is Charlie happy about the school that Sam is going to?

4. Why is Charlie's sister lucky to get to go to her chosen school?

5. What message does Charlie take from *The Fountainhead*?

6. What is Charlie's psychiatrist interested in?

Letter Forty-Six (June 5, 1992)

Summary

School is over and everyone is happy.

Patrick plays Frank 'n Furter one last time and gives a great show. Charlie persuades his sister and her boyfriend to come to the show too.

The party at Craig's is great. Charlie's friends are happy to have finished school and are looking forward to college.

Charlie plays music to suit the mood of the party. He cannot wait to see his brother, who is coming home for his sister's graduation.

Questions

1. Does it sound like Charlie is having a good time with his friends?
   What creates this feeling?

2. How does Charlie help his sister and her boyfriend when they come to the show?

3. Does his sister being there add anything to the mood of this letter, do you think?

4. What is the party at Craig's like?

5. How well is Charlie getting along with his brother and sister?

6. How is Charlie feeling these days?

7. What is the mood like as the letter ends?

Letter Forty-Seven (June 9, 1992)

Summary

Yesterday was difficult for Charlie, without his friends at school. He is afraid that now they will be too busy to spend time with him.

He hopes that senior prom is great for all of them.

Questions

1. What made yesterday difficult for Charlie?

2. How is Charlie feeling?

3. What does he worry about?

4. What hopes does Charlie have for senior prom? What does this tell you about him?

Letter Forty-Eight (June 10, 1992)

Summary

Charlie's sister is still asleep after prom, as are Patrick and Sam.

Charlie had two finals today.

Bill has invited him over to his house to spend Saturday afternoon with him and his girlfriend.

Graduation will take place on Sunday.

School is very lonely for Charlie.

Questions

1. Where will Charlie spend Saturday afternoon?

2. What will his weekend be like?

3. Why is Charlie planning so far ahead?

4. How is Charlie getting on with his schoolwork?

5. Do you feel like this story is coming to an end? Is it being neatly wrapped up? Explain your point of view.

Letter Forty-Nine (June 13, 1992)

Summary

Charlie hears that the prom was good.

Sam and Craig break up because he is cheating on her. Mary Elizabeth's boyfriend, Peter, makes Craig tell Sam the truth. He says if Craig does not tell her, then he will.

Craig talks to her in the bedroom and Sam leaves in tears. Craig and Peter scream at each other, and Patrick and Charlie drop Peter home.

Charlie knows he really loves Sam when he realises he is not happy about the break-up as Sam is hurt.

Bill thanks Charlie at lunch on Saturday afternoon because teaching him has been a wonderful experience. He tells Charlie that he is one of the most gifted people he has ever known.

Bill lets Charlie know that he will be there next year if he needs him. Charlie starts to cry, and Bill lets him be.

Nobody since his Aunt Helen has called Charlie special, and he is grateful to have heard it again.

Questions

1. What was the prom like?

2. What was the after-prom party like?

3. Why do Sam and Craig break up?
   What is your response to this?

4. What makes Craig tell Sam the truth?

5. Should Peter have interfered like this?
   Explain your point of view.

6. Describe Sam's reaction to the break-up.

7. What is the worst part, according to Charlie?
   What makes him say this?

8. Why is Charlie glad he stays at Craig's after Sam leaves?

9. What is your view of Craig after all of this?

10. What is your view of Peter?

11. What makes Charlie realise that he really loves Sam?
    Do you agree with him?

12. What is Bill's house like?

13. Why does Bill thank Charlie?
    What is your reaction to this?

14. Why did Bill give Charlie all the extra work?
    Does this surprise you?

15. Why is Bill telling Charlie this now?
    What is your response to this?

16. "He just let me hear what he had to say in my own way and let things be."
    Do Charlie and Bill have a good relationship?
    Explain your point of view.

17. Is Bill an important person in Charlie's life?

18. Was this a good afternoon for Charlie, do you think?

19. In this chapter, Bill tells Charlie that he is special, something he has not heard since his aunt Helen said it. Is it important to hear things like this about yourself? Give reasons for your answer.

Letter Fifty (June 16, 1992)

Summary

Charlie rides the bus home from school on the last day and thinks about how different everyone looks.

His brother is home from college and has grown a beard. He does not talk about himself, but is interested in what everyone is doing, especially his sister's graduation.

Charlie tells his family what the sports presenter in the park said about his brother. He freezes when he remembers where he met him, but gets away without saying more.

All of Charlie's extended family come to brunch the next morning for his sister's graduation.

Charlie's grandfather passes remarks about the number of black students at their school, until Charlie's brother threatens to drive him back to his nursing home.

Charlie's mother cries at his sister's speech and holds hands with him and his brother.

Charlie sees his sister and all of his friends get their diplomas.
Sam calls Charlie during his sister's party. His father says that he cannot leave until their relatives have gone.

Charlie drives downtown and meets his friends in a dance club. He dances with Sam and wishes the clock would stop.

Afterwards, they go to Peter's apartment and Charlie gives everyone their graduation presents.

He gives his books from Bill to Sam and Patrick, as they are his favourite people in the world.

It hits Charlie that they are all leaving and he begins to cry. Sam makes a deal with him that when they are lonely, they will call each other.

The next day the teachers let the students sit around and talk, but Charlie does not really know anyone, so has nobody to talk to.

He is glad that school is over so he can spend time with his friends before they leave.

He got straight A's all year.

Questions

1. What is different about Charlie's brother?

2. What causes Charlie to panic at dinner?
   How does he get away with his blunder here?

3. How do Charlie's family celebrate his sister's graduation?
   Is this event important to them, do you think?

4. How does Charlie's brother control his grandfather?

5. How does Charlie's mother react to his sister's speech?
   What does this tell you about her?

6. Does Charlie have a loving family?
   Explain your point of view, using examples from the text.

7. What is the party for Charlie's sister like?

8. Why can't Charlie leave after Sam calls?
   What is your response to this?

9. How does Charlie describe the tunnel that leads downtown at night?

10. Are you surprised that Sam dances with Charlie in the dance club?
    What is going on here?

11. What gifts does Charlie give Sam and Patrick?
    What is your response to this?

12. What makes Charlie start to cry?

13. What deal does Sam make with Charlie?
    Will this help Charlie, do you think?

14. How do they spend the rest of the night?

15. What is school like for Charlie the next day?
    How does this make you feel?

16. How does Bill make things a bit better?

17. Why is Charlie glad that the school year is over?

18. Are you worried about how Charlie will get on when he returns to school?
    Give reasons for your answer.

Letter Fifty-One (June 22, 1992)

Summary

Sam is busy getting ready to leave. She has lunch with Craig, giving her closure on their relationship.

The group spends the night before Sam leaves remembering all the good times they have had together.

The others leave and Charlie keeps Sam company as she packs.

She asks him why he never asked her out when she broke up with Craig. She tells him that he needs to stop putting everybody else's life ahead of his own.

She plans to do what she wants and be herself from now on.

Sam asks Charlie what he wants and needs and he kisses her. They touch each other and undress. When she moves her hand under his pants, he stops her. She is very nice to him, but he gets really upset and wants to go home.

He spends the night on the couch at Sam's. He dreams he is watching television with his Aunt Helen and she is doing to him what Sam was doing earlier that night.

When Sam and Patrick leave the next morning, Charlie goes home instead of going with the others. He cannot talk to anyone and is thinking too fast again.

He thanks 'Dear friend' for being someone who listens and apologises for wasting their time.

Questions

1. How is Sam the week before she leaves?

2. How does Sam's lunch with Craig go?

3. How do they spend the night before Sam leaves?

4. "I just remember walking between them and feeling for the first time that I belonged somewhere."
   What insight does this give you into Charlie and his life?
   How important are his friendships with Sam and Patrick?

5. What advice does Sam give Charlie?

6. How does Charlie feel when Sam tells him that he was not honest with Patrick?
   Is she right in what she says?

7. What does Sam plan to do when she leaves?

8. Like Bill, Sam says that Charlie does not really participate in life.
   Are they right?

9. How does Charlie respond when Sam asks him what he wants to do?

10. When does Charlie stop Sam from touching him?
    How does he feel?
    What is going on, do you think?

11. "I can't do that anymore. I'm sorry."
    Who could Charlie be speaking to here?

12. What dream does Charlie have?
    What does this mean?
    What is your reaction to this?

13. What does Charlie do when Patrick and Sam leave?

14. What does he realise about his Aunt Helen?

15. What does he think about the little kid eating french fries?

16. What does Charlie tell his "Dear friend" before signing off?
    How does this make you feel?

Epilogue: Letter Fifty-Two (August 23, 1992)

Summary

Charlie is just out of hospital, where he has been for two months. His parents found him naked in his living room, in a trance that he could not snap out of.

He answered the doctor's questions in the hospital and realised that what he dreamt about his Aunt Helen was true.

Having visitors in the hospital helped him a lot, as did getting cards and mail.

Charlie's brother and sister asked him a lot of questions about Aunt Helen.

He does not blame her for what she did to him.

Charlie is glad to be out of hospital and with his family again.

He goes to the Big Boy with Sam and Patrick. Afterwards, they drive through the tunnel.

He thinks about all of the good things that people have said to him over the past year and is grateful for his family and friends.

He cries and smiles in the tunnel, and is really there.

Charlie begins his sophomore year of high school tomorrow. He is not that afraid of going. He says that if this is his last letter, believe that things are good with him.

Questions

1. Where has Charlie been for the last two months?
   Why was he sent there?
   What is your response to this?

2. What has Charlie realised about his Aunt Helen?
   Looking back on the story, does this explain anything, do you think?

3. How do Charlie's parents react to this news?

4. What helps Charlie the most in hospital?

5. Are Charlie's family and friends supportive?

6. When does he start to feel like everything is going to be alright?

7. Does Charlie blame his Aunt Helen?
   What outlook does he have?

8. "...if I ever have kids, and they are upset, I won't tell them that there are people starving in China or anything like that..."
   Do you agree with Charlie's outlook here?
   Comment on how Charlie feels to be at home.

9. Where does Charlie go with Patrick and Sam?

10. How does Charlie feel, in the back of the pickup as they drive through the tunnel?

11. How do you feel, reading the end of this story? Are you hopeful for Charlie's future?

12. Is this a good ending, in your opinion? Explain your point of view.

13. What is the mood like, as the story ends?

Further Questions

1. Did you enjoy the ending of this novel? Why/why not?
   What questions are you left with?

2. Does this story teach us anything about people?
   Does it teach us anything about life?
   Refer to the text to support the points you make.

3. Did you become emotionally involved in this story?
   Why is this the case?

4. Is Charlie a good narrator?
   Do you like how this story is told?

5. Who is your favourite character in this novel?
   What do you like about them?

6. Who is your least favourite character in this novel?
   What do you dislike about them?

7. What are the major themes and issues in this text?
   How are they explored?
   What conclusions do you draw?

8. What did you enjoy about this story?

9. What did you dislike about this story?

10. Is this novel engaging and entertaining? Explain your point of view.

11. Is this a sad story? Explain your point of view

12. Is this an accurate account of teenage life? Use examples to support the points that you make.

13. Is there a lesson or moral to this story?

14. This novel was banned in some schools for its content. Why, exactly, do you think was it banned?

Theme/Issue (HL) ~ Relationships (OL)

Relationships has been selected as the theme/issue to explore in relation to this text.

The theme of relationships can be applied to any relationship in a text and includes love, marriage, friendship and family bonds. Consider the complexities of relationships and the impact they have on characters' lives.

1. What is the relationship between Charlie and his "Dear friend"?

2. Is Charlie close to his family?
   Support your points with examples from the text.

3. Does Charlie's sister have a good relationship with her (secret) boyfriend?
   Use examples to support the points you make.

4. Are Charlie's mother and father good parents?
   Use examples to illustrate your viewpoint.

5. Is Charlie close to his parents?
   Does he love them?
   Do they love him?
   Include examples in your answer.

6. Do Charlie and his family communicate well?
   Does this improve or hinder the family's relationships?

7. Comment on the secrecy surrounding Brad and Patrick's relationship.
   Do they care about one another, do you think?

8. On February 15, the night of the dance, Charlie's sister tells him she is pregnant.
   What does this episode reveal to you about Charlie's relationship with his sister?

9. What improves Charlie's relationship with his sister? Why is this the case?

10. Charlie's father and sister each offer him advice about Mary Elizabeth.
    What does this suggest about his family?

11. Charlie is a very open character.
    Does his openness improve his relationships with others? Explain your point of view.

12. Does secrecy characterise relationships in this text? Explain your point of view.

13. Does Charlie have a good relationship with Sam?
    Include examples in your answer.

14. Does Charlie have a good relationship with Patrick?
    Include examples in your answer.

15. Does Charlie have a good relationship with his brother?
    Include examples in your answer.

16. Does Charlie have a good relationship with his sister?
    Include examples in your answer.

17. Are Charlie's friends important to him?

18. Why do Charlie's friends isolate him?
    Why do they take him back?
    Are they 'real' friends?
    Explain your point of view fully.

19. Do Charlie's parents have good relationships with their own families?
    How does this add to the theme of relationships in the novel?

20. Describe Charlie's relationship with his aunt Helen.
    What problems do you see in this relationship?
    How has his relationship with his aunt affected him?
    How has his relationship with his aunt affected his relationships with other people?

21. Describe Charlie's relationship with Bill, his advanced english teacher.
    Is this relationship significant?
    How does it add to the theme of relationships in this novel?

22. What is the most significant relationship in this story?
    What makes this relationship stand out for you?
    What does it tell us about human relationships, friendship and love?

23. Are relationships in this story positive or negative? What makes them this way?

24. Are a lot of the relationships in this novel characterised by conflict? Explain your point of view.

25. What else characterises relationships in this text? (Are they generally supportive, secretive, honest, loving, etc.?)

26. Do relationships in this story bring characters happiness or sorrow? Include examples in your answer.

27. Do characters in this text have a realistic view of love? Explain, using examples from the text to support the points that you make.

28. What makes relationships difficult in this text?

29. What helps relationships in this text?

30. How do relationships change during the story?

31. What do you learn about relationships from reading this novel?

32. Are relationships portrayed realistically in this text? Make use of examples to support the points that you make.

33. Are relationships in this story interesting and involving? Explain your point of view, using examples to illustrate your ideas.

34. Does any aspect of the theme of relationships in this text shock, upset or unsettle you?
Use examples to help explain your point of view.

Literary Genre (HL)

Literary Genre refers to the way the story is told. Consider aspects of narration such as the manner and style of narration, characterisation, setting, tension, literary techniques, etc.

1. What does the letter format add to this story? (How does it affect the tone, perspective, pacing of the story?)

2. Does Charlie's series of letters form a connection with the reader?
   Why/why not?

3. What are your first impressions of Charlie, the speaker?

4. What intrigues you about Charlie in Part One?

5. How does the writer draw on memory and use flashbacks to build your view of Charlie and develop the storyline?

6. This story takes place over the course of a year.
   What does the timeframe of this novel add to the story?

7. There are a number of darker moments and episodes in this novel.
   Identify these moments and suggest what they add to the story.

8. There are a number of lighter moments and episodes in this novel.
Identify these moments and suggest what they add to the story.

9. Is there humour in this story?
Where do you see it?
What does it add to the story?

10. Does this novel sound authentic and true to you?
Use examples to support your case.

11. What does the author's use of conflict add to this novel?
Include examples in your answer.

12. In his penultimate letter, dated June 22, 1992, Charlie addresses his "Dear friend", talking about *them*, as he has not done since the beginning of the novel.
What is the effect of this?
What impact does this have on the storytelling?

13. When you learn what Aunt Helen has done to Charlie, does your understanding of Charlie, his behaviour and events in the novel, change also?
Explain, using examples.
Does revealing this information in this way add to the story?
Explain your point of view.

14. Are characters complex or one-dimensional in this text?
What is the effect of this on the story?
Include examples in your answer.

15. Chbosky rarely describes how characters look. What is the effect tof this?

16. Do you like the way this story is told?
Include examples in your answer.

17. Does this novel have a satisfying ending?
Explain your point of view.

18. Comment on the mood as the story ends.

19. Does the reader always know exactly what is going on in this novel?
Explain your viewpoint.
How does the author achieve this?
What is the effect of this?

20. How does setting contribute to the story?

21. Do you find this novel to be interesting and easy to read?
Include examples in your answer.

22. What draws the reader into this story?
Highlight specific aspects of the text in your answer.

23. How does the author create a darkness in the story at times?

24. Identify the various sources of conflict in this text.
How does conflict add to the story?

25. What are the high points of this novel?
What makes them exciting and intriguing?

26. Did you enjoy the storyline of the text?
    Was it exciting, compelling, tense or emotional?
    Use examples from the text to support your answer.

27. Is there just one plot or many plots?
    What connections can you make between these storylines?

28. What interested you most in the story?

29. Are characters vivid, realistic and well-developed?
    Explain your point of view, using examples from the text.

30. Who is your favourite character in this novel?
    What makes you like/admire them?

31. Who is your least favourite character in this novel?
    What makes you dislike them?

32. Do you empathise or identify with any characters?

33. What themes can you identify in this story?

34. Does this novel have a 'real life' quality to it?
    If so, how is this achieved?
    What does this add to the story?

35. Is this a sad story?
    Explain your point of view.

36. How does the author create an emotional response in his reader?
    What techniques does he use to good advantage?

37. Consider the author's use of tension and resolution in the novel.
    What are the major tensions/problems/conflicts in the text?
    Are they resolved or not?

38. Does the author make use of any striking patterns of imagery or symbols to add to this story?

39. How does the aythor make use of the unexpected?
    What does this add to the story?

40. What is the climax (high point) of the story?
    What do you think of this moment?
    How does it make you feel?

41. Comment on the language of the novel.

42. What do you find moving or emotional in this novel?

43. What aspects of the novel form worked well in this story, in your view?

44. What do you like about the way this story is told?

45. Did this novel grip you as a reader and hold your attention?

46. To what genre does this novel belong?
    Support your choice with examples from the text.

47. *The Perks of Being a Wallflower* is a 'coming-of-age' novel. What does this mean?

General Vision and Viewpoint (HL)

General Vision and Viewpoint refers to the author's outlook or view of life and how this viewpoint is represented in the text.

1. In the opening letter, the speaker talks about his friend's suicide.
   How does this impact on the atmosphere of the story?

2. In Letter Eight (October 14, 1991), Charlie's sister calls him a freak and adds that everyone says so.
   How do her comments contribute to the General Vision and Viewpoint of the novel?

3. Charlie remembers a rape taking place at his brother's party.
   How does this memory affect the mood and outlook of this story?

4. What does the secrecy surrounding Patrick's relationship with Brad suggest about life?

5. Charlie's family do not talk about the 'bad thing' that happened his Aunt Helen.
   His mother does not let him talk about what is upsetting him at Christmas.
   How do these silences contribute to the General Vision and Viewpoint of this text?

6. Helen's dad did not believe she was molested and her abuser continued to visit her family.
How does this add to the General Vision and Viewpoint of the novel?

7. Does Charlie strike you as a lonely character?
How does this make you feel?
How does his loneliness influence the General Vision and Viewpoint of the text?

8. How does conflict impact on the General Vision and Viewpoint of this story?
Refer to examples in your answer.

9. Is there a lot of sadness in this story?
Explain, including examples.

10. Is there a lot of happiness in this story?
Explain, including examples.

11. How does isolation impact on the General Vision and Viewpoint of this story?
Refer to examples in your answer.

12. Charlie's sister relies on him to accompany her to the clinic to have her pregnancy terminated.
What does Charlie's compassion and understanding suggest about life?

13. Charlie waits for his sister while her pregnancy is terminated. Afterwards, they laugh together.
What does their laughter, despite their situation, suggest?

14. What is life like for Charlie, when he is cut off from his friends?
How does this affect the story's General Vision and Viewpoint?

15. How does Patrick feel, after Brad jeers him in school?
What does this incident in the cafeteria reveal to you about life?

16. Are there many dark or bleak moments in this novel?
What does this suggest about the author's view of life?

17. What does graduation represent for these characters?
How does graduation add to the atmosphere?

18. How does Bill's interest in Charlie colour the mood of this story?

19. How does the reality of what Aunt Helen did to Charlie affect the General Vision and Viewpoint?

20. Does Charlie face many obstacles in life?
Does he overcome these obstacles and struggles?
How do they affect his attitude?
What does this suggest about life?

21. Despite the problems he has had, has Charlie enjoyed himself and been enriched by the events of this novel?
What does this tell us about the author's attitude to life?

22. Does this story end on a hopeful or hopeless note?
What does this suggest about the author's view of life?

23. Are characters in this text hopeful and forward looking about life?
    Are they realistic? Do they make well-thought out plans?
    What does this suggest about their outlook on life?

24. What comments do characters make on their society and the problems they are facing?

25. Are characters happy or unhappy?

26. What makes characters in this story happy and fulfilled?

27. What makes characters in this story unhappy and unfulfilled?

28. Are relationships destructive or nurturing?
    What do they reveal about life as we see characters supported/thwarted in their efforts to grow/mature?

29. Is life full of possibility and potential in this text?

30. Are imagery and language bright or dark in the text? (Tone of the text)

31. What is the mood of this text?
    Include examples to justify your ideas.

32. What does this novel suggest about the power of friendship?

33. What does this novel suggest about human nature?
    Is this outlook positive or negative?

34. Do characters face many obstacles and difficulties in this text? Do they struggle?
    Why/why not?

35. Is this text dark and bleak or uplifting and inspiring?
    Give reasons for your view.

36. Is there a lesson or moral to this story?
    What could it be?

37. What does this story teach us about life?

38. How do you feel as you read the novel?
    Refer to key moments to anchor your answer.

39. Does the novel end on a hopeful, optimistic note, or a hopeless, pessimistic one?
    Are questions raised by the text resolved by the end?
    Are they resolved happily or unhappily?
    How do you feel at the end?
    Explain your point of view.

40. Are you hopeful or despairing regarding the prospects for human happiness in this story?
    (Are characters likely to be happy?)

41. Identify the aspects of life that the author concentrates on.
    Are they positive or negative?
    What is he telling us by focusing on these aspects of life?

42. Identify bright, hopeful, optimistic aspects of the novel.

43. Identify dark, hopeless, pessimistic aspects of the novel.

44. Does this novel offer a comforting or disturbing view of life?
Overall, is it optimistic or pessimistic?
Explain your point of view.

45. Can you relate any aspect of this text to your own life experience?
If so, how does this help to shape your understanding of the General Vision and Viewpoint of this text?

Cultural Context (HL)/Social Setting (OL)

Cultural Context refers to the world of the text.
Consider social norms, beliefs, values and attitudes.

Social Setting refers to the setting, time and place, etc. where the story takes place.

1. When and where does this story take place?

2. Charlie opens his story by recounting his reaction to his friend's suicide.
   What insight does this give you into this world?

3. Charlie's sister goes out with a boy when he hits her.
   Why does she do this?
   What does this tell you about this world?

4. Is this a violent place?
   Use examples in your answer.

5. In Letter Ten (October 28, 1991), Charlie remembers a couple in his room at a party.
   How does the boy treat the girl?
   What is your response to this?
   What insight does this incident give you into the world of this text?

6. In Letter Ten (October 28, 1991) Charlie says that Patrick and Brad do not speak at the homecoming dance and that his sister dances with the boy she is not allowed see. What do each of these details tell you about this world?

7. Patrick was secretly seeing Brad at parties for months. What does his behaviour here suggest about the Cultural Contex/Social Setting of this text?

8. What insight does Brad's drug and alcohol use give you into this world?

9. Charlie's siblings argue in the car on Christmas day. What issues do they disagree about? What insight does their conversation give you into their world and society?

10. What does Charlie's drug use reveal about this world? Is it difficult for Charlie to get drugs? Is his drug use a problem for Charlie?

11. Is this world a lonely place? Give reasons for your answer.

12. Charlie's sister is upset when she finds out she is pregnant. What does this reveal to you about her world?

13. Charlie's sister's boyfriend breaks up with her when she tells him she is pregnant, saying that the baby is not his. What does his reaction reveal about this world and the treatment of women?

14. What does the fight in the cafeteria reveal about this world?

15. What does Patrick's relationship with Brad tell you about the society of the novel?

16. What do Bill's words to Charlie on the afternoon in his apartment tell you about this world?

17. Are people treated fairly in this world? Is it a just place?

18. Helen's father did not believe she was molested.
    Brad's father did not believe he was gay.
    What does this disbelief tell you about the world of this text?

19. Do parents in this novel love, esteem and value their children?
    Explain, using examples.

20. Can characters rely on and trust each other in the world of this text?

21. What characterises the Cultural Context/Social Setting of this novel as being distinctly 90s?

22. Do the characters in this novel drink a lot and do a lot of drugs?
    Is it easy for them to get alcohol and drugs?
    What attitude do they have to these substances?
    What does this attitude reveal about this world?

23. Is it difficult to be gay in this world?
What does this tell you about this place?

24. Is this world a very adult place?
What stresses and pressures do the teenagers have to cope with?

25. Do men mistreat women in this world?
Support your answer with examples from the story.

26. What time and place is this story set in?

27. Is this world a romantic place?
Explain your point of view.

28. Are wealth and class important in this world?
What view do characters have towards money and class?

29. Is race important in this world?

30. Are characters in this text moral and upstanding?

31. What do characters value in this story?

32. What kind of society do you see in this text?
(How do people treat one another? What do they believe in? What is important to them?)

33. Is there violence and conflict in this world?
Where do you see this violence and conflict?

34. Is this a secure or dangerous world?

35. What is the role of women in the world of this novel?

36. How are women viewed and treated in this story?

37. Is family important in the world of this text?

38. What is the most important thing to characters in this world?
    What is your response to this?

39. Are characters in this world free to live as they choose, or must they conform to society's expectations?

40. Is this world a supportive or destructive environment for the novel's characters?

41. Are friendship and love important in this world, or are characters self-centred and self-serving?
    Justify your viewpoint with reference to the text.

42. Is the world of this text a happy or sad place?
    Use examples to justify your viewpoint.

43. This novel covers a year of Charlie's life.
    Is it a realistic portrayal of a year in the life of a teenager?
    Explain your point of view.

44. Would you like to live in the world of *The Perks of Being a Wallflower*?
    Include examples to justify your viewpoint.

Hero, Heroine, Villain (OL)

'Hero, Heroine, Villain' refers to central characters (protagonists/antagonists).

Their traits, values, etc. and their ability to deal with conflict, challenges, obstacles, etc. should be considered.

Charlie

1. What strengths do you see in Charlie's character?

2. What weaknesses do you see in Charlie's character?

3. Is Charlie an emotional character?
   Refer to the text to support your view.
   Is he too emotional at times?
   Explain your answer.

4. Does Charlie love Sam?
   Is he a romantic figure?

5. Is Charlie loyal?
   Refer to the text to support your view.

6. Is Charlie honest?
   Refer to the text to support your view.

7. Is Charlie brave?
   Refer to the text to support your view.

8. Is Charlie lonely?
   Refer to the text to support your view.

9. Are Charlie's friends important to him?
   Why do you think this is the case?

10. What makes Charlie struggle in the world of this novel?

11. What does Charlie value?

12. How well does Charlie cope with conflict?

13. How well does Charlie cope with obstacles/challenges?

14. Is Charlie a happy and content character?
    Explain your viewpoint fully.

15. What makes Charlie an interesting character in your opinion?
    Why do readers like him, do you think?

16. If you could chat to Charlie, what would you talk about?
    What advice would you give him?
    What questions would you ask?

17. Would you be friends with Charlie, do you think?
    Give reasons for your answer.

The Comparative Study: Comparing Texts

Use the following questions to compare your texts, noting the similarities and differences between them. Include examples to support the points that you make.

Theme/Issue - Relationships

1. Are relationships in this text more positive and supportive than the relationships in your other chosen texts?
   Include specific examples in your answer.

2. Rank the relationships you have studied in your various texts from most positive (score of 10) to most negative (score of 1).
   Add a note explaining your choices.

3. Are relationships in this text the most engaging and interesting that you have studied?
   Explain your choice.

4. Rank the relationships you have studied in your various texts from the most interesting (score of 10) to the least

interesting (score of 1).
Add a note explaining your choices.

5. Did you learn most about the theme of relationships from this text or another text on your Comparative Study course?
Refer to your chosen texts to support your answer.

6. How do the events of the text impact on the characters' relationships with one another in this text and your other chosen texts?
Who is most affected?
Who is least affected?

7. How does conflict impact on the relationships of characters in this text and your other chosen texts?
Who is most affected?
Who is least affected?

8. How does social class impact on the relationships of characters in this text and your other chosen texts?
Who is most affected?
Who is least affected?

9. Is the theme of relationships portrayed in an idealistic or realistic way in each of your chosen texts?

10. Did any aspect of the theme of relationships shock or surprise you in your three chosen texts?
Use examples from your texts to support the points that you make.

11. What are the most interesting aspects of the theme of relationships in each of your chosen texts?

12. Which text taught you most about relationships? Refer to each text in your answer.

13. What key moments best capture the theme of relationships in each of your texts?

14. What similarities do you notice in the theme of relationships in this text and your other Comparative Study texts?

15. What differences do you notice in the theme of relationships in this text and your other Comparative Study texts?

Literary Genre

1. Did you like the way this story was told more than your other Comparative Study texts?
State what you enjoyed most (and least) about each.

2. Is this text more exciting than your other texts? Consider tension, suspense, pacing, conflict and the author's use of the unexpected.

3. How does the author make use of tension in each of your chosen texts?
Where is it most effective?
Where is it least effective?
Use examples to support your point of view.

4. How does the author make use of climax in each of your chosen texts?
Where is it most effective?
Where is it least effective?
Use examples to support your point of view.

5. How does the author make use of resolution in each of your chosen texts?
Where is it most effective?
Where is it least effective?
Use examples to support your point of view.

6. Are characters more engaging in this text than in your other texts?
Refer to each of your texts in your answer.

7. How does the author create vivid, memorable characters in each of your chosen texts?

8. In which of your texts are characters most life-like and compelling?
In which text are characters least life-like and most difficult to relate to?
Refer to each of your texts in your answer.

9. Is the setting more effective in telling the story in this text, than in your other texts?

10. Is setting more central to the story in this text or another text you have studied as part of your Comparative Study?

11. Is this text more unpredictable than your other texts? Refer to each of your texts in your answer.

12. Does this text have greater emotional power than your other texts?
Was this emotional power created in a more interesting way here or in a different text?
Refer to each of your texts in your answer.

13. What was your favourite literary technique, used by the author of each of your texts?
How did the use of this technique help the storytelling?

14. To what extent are you influenced by the point of view that this story is told from?
Are you influenced to a greater or lesser degree by the point of view utilised in your other Comparative Study texts?

15. What key moments best capture Literary Genre in each of your texts?

16. What similarities do you notice in the Literary Genre of this text and your other Comparative Study texts?
Mention specific aspects of narrative.

17. What differences do you notice in the Literary Genre of this text and your other Comparative Study texts?
Mention specific aspects of narrative.

General Vision and Viewpoint

1. Is life happier and fuller for characters in this text than in your other Comparative Study texts?
Explain your point of view fully.

2. Do characters in this text face more obstacles and difficulties than in your other texts?
Who struggles most?

3. Are characters in this text rewarded more for their struggles than in your other texts?
Do they overcome adversity and achieve true happiness and contentment in a way that is not realised in your other texts?

4. How do events in these texts, and your personal response to these events, help your understanding of the General Vision and Viewpoint of these texts?
Include specific examples in your answer.

5. How does your attitude to central characters help shape your understanding of the General Vision and Viewpoint of your chosen texts?

Include specific reference to your chosen characters in your answer.

6. What aspects of this text did you respond to emotionally? How does this help your understanding of the General Vision and Viewpoint of the text?
How does this compare to your other texts?

7. Is this the brightest, most hopeful and triumphant text you have studied?
Explain why its message is more or less positive than in your other texts.

8. Which of your chosen texts was the bleakest and most upsetting or depressing?
Explain what made it more negative than your other texts. What made them more positive?

9. Plot your three texts on a scale of one to ten from darkest (most pessimistic) to brightest (most optimistic). Add a note to explain their positions.

10. Which key moments best capture the General Vision and Viewpoint of each of your texts?

11. What similarities do you notice in the General Vision and Viewpoint of this text and your other Comparative Study texts?

12. What differences do you notice in the General Vision and Viewpoint of this text and your other Comparative Study texts?

Cultural Context/Social Setting

Consider each of your chosen texts in your answers.

1. In which of the texts you have studied for the Comparative Study do characters have the most freedom and choice?
   Justify your answer with examples from your chosen texts.

2. In which of your texts are characters most controlled?

3. Who holds the power in each world?
   Who is powerless?

4. In which of your texts do characters have the most freedom?
   Why is this the case?

5. In which world is difference most accepted and respected?
   In which world is difference least accepted and respected?

6. Which world is the least tolerant?
   Which world is the most tolerant?
   Include examples to explain your view.

7. Which world is the best to live in if you are a woman?
   Give reasons for your answer.

8. Which world is the best to live in if you are a man?
   Give reasons for your answer.

9. Which world is the best to live in if you are a child? Give reasons for your answer.

10. Which text portrays the most violent and volatile world?

11. Which of your texts portrays the safest, most secure place?

12. Which of your texts portrays the most supportive world?

13. Which of these worlds is the darkest, most fearful place?

14. Which of these worlds is the brightest, most joyful place?

15. Which of these places is the most unpredictable?

16. Which text portrays the most traditional world?

17. Which of these societies holds family in the highest esteem?

18. Which of these societies holds love in the highest esteem? Which of these societies holds love in the lowest esteem?

19. Which of these societies holds power in the highest esteem?

20. Which of these societies holds wealth in the highest esteem?

21. Where do you see the best treatment of the vulnerable of society? Refer to each of your texts and include examples.

22. Where do you see the worst treatment of the vulnerable of society?
Refer to each of your texts and include examples.

23. Which of the worlds you have studied is the most materialistic?
Which of the worlds you have studied is the least materialistic?
What makes characters have these outlooks?

24. Which of the worlds you have studied is the most secretive?
What makes characters behave this way?

25. Which of your texts displays the greediest world?
What makes characters have this attitude?

26. Where is love most important?
Where is love most successful?
Where is love least important?
Where is love least succesful?
Compare the success of love in each of your chosen texts.
What does this tell you about the worlds of these texts and characters' lives?

27. Which of these worlds appealed to you most?
Give reasons for your answer.

28. Which of these worlds appealed to you least?
Explain your point of view.

29. Which of your texts is home to the most religious or spiritual world?

30. Which of your texts showed the least religious or spiritual society?

31. How important is social class in each of your texts?

32. In which of your texts are characters most accepting of their world and society?

33. In which of your texts do characters challenge their world, society and values most?

34. In which of your texts do you see the greatest inequality?

35. In which of your texts do you see the greatest injustice?

36. Where do characters behave the best towards one another?
How does Cultural Context/Social Setting influence their behaviour?

37. How do characters reflect the Cultural Context/Social Setting of their worlds?
Explain, including examples.

38. How does the Cultural Context/Social Setting of your texts lead to problems and difficulties for the texts' characters?
How does it affect characters' responses to these difficulties?

39. What key moments best capture the Cultural Context/ Social Setting of each of your texts?

40. What similarities do you notice in the Cultural Context/ Social Setting of this text and your other Comparative Study texts?

41. What differences do you notice in the Cultural Context/ Social Setting of this text and your other Comparative Study texts?

Hero/Heroine/Villain

Consider the following list of questions for a central character in each of your chosen texts.

1. Who is the most interesting character in the text?
   What makes them interesting?
   What do you like about them?
   What do you dislike about them?
   What are this character's strengths?
   What are this character's weaknesses?

2. How does this character cope with conflict?

3. How does this character cope with the unexpected?

4. Are they a resourceful character?

5. Are they an emotional character?
Use examples to support your view.

6. Do you empathise with this character? Why/why not?

7. What do you admire about this character?

8. How well does this character relate to and interact with other characters?
Include examples to support your points.

9. Is this character happy or sad?

10. Are they an active or passive character?
How do they contribute to the action and storyline of the text?
Are they important to the story's plot and development?

11. Is this character a good (successful and interesting) main character?

12. Would you like to meet this character?
If you met them, what would you talk about?

13. If you had any advice for this character, what would it be?

14. Does this character make the story more exciting?
In what way do they do this?

15. Is this character a hero/heroine or a villain?
Explain your choice.

16. On a scale of one to ten (with one being extremely heroic and ten being an evil villain), where would you place your chosen character?
    Give reasons for your choice.
    Where would you place the main characters from your other texts?
    Why would you place them here?

17. Identify the key moments in the text that illustrate your chosen character's personality traits/character.

18. Which of your chosen characters do you like and admire most?
    What makes them your favourite character?
    Give reasons for your answer.

19. Which of your chosen characters do you dislike most?
    Explain why you like some more than others.

20. Which of your chosen characters shocked you most?
    Give reasons for your answer.

21. Which of your chosen characters impressed you most?
    Give reasons for your answer.

22. Which of your chosen characters did you feel most sorry for?
    Give reasons for your answer.

23. Who is the most resourceful character you have come across?
    Give reasons for your answer.

24. Which of your chosen characters faced the most problems and difficulties?
    Did they cope well with these problems?

25. How is your favourite character similar to the characters in your other texts?

26. How is your favourite character different to the characters in your other texts?

27. Choose key moments from each of your texts to highlight your main characters' strengths and weaknesses.

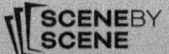

www.ingramcontent.com/pod-product-compliance
Lightning Source LLC
Chambersburg PA
CBHW071450080526
44587CB00014B/2056